Visit Tyndale's exciting Web site at www.tyndale.com

Photography by Zul Mukhida
Concept by Rachel O'Neil
Design by Gloria Chantell
Special thanks to Ron Kaufmann

Published by Tyndale House Publishers, Inc.
351 Executive Drive
Carol Stream, Illinois 60188

ISBN hardcover: 0-8423-3673-7
ISBN softcover: 0-8423-5193-0

2 4 6 8 10 9 7 5 3 1

Printed in Belgium

THE CHRISTMAS STAR

Soft sculptures by Christine Potter

Story adapted from original text by Moira Butterfield

TYNDALE HOUSE PUBLISHERS, INC., WHEATON, ILLINOIS

Long ago, the emperor wanted to know how many people there were in the whole Roman Empire. So he ordered everyone to travel to the places where their families came from so they could be counted.

A carpenter named Joseph and his wife, Mary, lived in Nazareth. They had to travel to the town of Bethlehem in Judea, where Joseph's family came from.

Mary was going to have a baby. An angel told Mary and Joseph that this baby would be very special. He would be God's own Son, Jesus! God had chosen Mary to be the mother of his one and only child.

By the time Mary and Joseph arrived in Bethlehem, the little town was already very crowded with people who had come to be counted.

Joseph tried to find a place where he and Mary could sleep. But there wasn't even one tiny room left at the inn.

Finally they found a stable filled with animals. Mary and Joseph would have to share the stable with cows and donkeys and sheep, but there was plenty of clean hay to sleep on. And the stable was warm and dry.

Mary and Joseph were happy to have a place to stay! And the kind, gentle animals didn't mind having them there at all.

Mary knew this was going to be a special night. The angel had said, "Your baby will be born a holy king, and his kingdom will last forever."

During the night, Mary's baby was born. She wrapped him up so he would be warm. Then she laid him in a manger filled with clean hay. The animals knew that something special had happened. But there was no way they could have known how special the tiny new baby really was.

That same night some shepherds were taking care of their sheep in a field near Bethlehem. As they looked up into the night sky, an angel suddenly appeared! And light shone brightly all around.

At first the shepherds were scared, but the angel spoke kindly to them.

"Don't be afraid," the angel said. "I have come to tell you some very happy news. Today the Savior has been born in Bethlehem. You will find him in a stable, lying in a manger."

Then the sky was filled with lots of angels, all singing God's praises.

After the angels went back to heaven, the shepherds said, "Come on, let's go to Bethlehem! Let's see this wonderful baby."

The shepherds hurried to Bethlehem and found the stable. When they looked inside, they saw baby Jesus in the manger, just as the angel had said.

"It's true!" they cried. "The Son of God is born!" How excited they all were! When they went back to their sheep, they told everyone about the baby and what the angel had said.

F ar away in the East, some wise men were watching the night sky when they saw a bright new star.

"This star means that a new king has been born," they said. "We must find him and worship him."

The wise men traveled over mountains and across deserts. They carried beautiful boxes with expensive treasures for the new king. The boxes held gifts of gold and sweet-smelling oils called frankincense and myrrh.

The wise men followed the bright new star to Bethlehem. Finally the star stopped right above a house.

"This must be the place we've been looking for," the wise men said. "The star has led us to the child God sent to be the new king."

The wise men were right, of course! They had come to the house where Mary, Joseph, and Jesus lived.

They went inside and found Mary holding God's Son, Jesus. They knelt down and worshiped the holy child. Then, one by one, they opened the beautiful boxes and laid their gifts at the feet of little Jesus.

The wise men knew that they had seen the new king God had sent from heaven. How happy they were that they had seen the special star!

But not everyone was happy about the birth of Jesus. When Herod, the king of Judea, heard the wise men say a new king was born, he was very angry. He didn't want any other king in his land.

"Find this child everyone is talking about," he shouted to his soldiers. "Don't let him grow up and become king!"

That night an angel came to Joseph in his dreams. The angel warned him to take his family far away to Egypt so they would be safe. Joseph woke Mary, and right away they left for Egypt with Jesus. When Herod's soldiers searched Bethlehem, the child Jesus was gone.

When it was safe again, Joseph brought his family to the town of Nazareth, where Jesus grew up healthy and strong.

We can be thankful that Jesus came to earth as a tiny baby. He brought God's love and forgiveness to the world—and to us! And every year we can remember the bright Christmas star as we celebrate Jesus' birthday.